The Black Fens

H.J. Mason

Published by Providence Press,
Providence Place, Wardy Hill, Ely, Cambridgeshire

Acknowledgement
The Publisher wishes to thank the Royal Geographical Society for permission to reproduce Major Gordon Fowler's map 'Fenland Waterways - Past and Present'.

First published as *An Introduction to the Black Fens* 1973
ISBN 0 903803 00 3
Reprinted 1974, 1976, 1979

Second edition 1984
ISBN 0 903803 12 7

Published by Providence Press, Providence Place,
Wardy Hill, Ely, Cambridgeshire

Produced by Millennia Limited, Hong Kong
Designed by Rosanne Chan
Printed and bound in Hong Kong
by South China Printing Co.

Contents

Introduction

Coveney, built on a fen 'island'

The East Anglian Fens can be divided into two distinct parts: to the north is the area of rich silt land and to the south is the area known as the Black Fens.

The area of rich silt land to the north is perhaps best known for its colourful fields of tulips and daffodils which, as a by-product of bulb production, provide flowers for the decorated floats in the Spalding spring festival parade. Around Boston crops include cauliflowers, early potatoes, onions and wheat, while near Wisbech much of the land is planted with orchards, many of which are Bramley apples; there are also fields of strawberries, rose bushes and nursery stock.

The area to the south is termed the Black Fens because of the dark soils derived from peat. Centred on that part of Cambridgeshire which was the former administrative county of the Isle of Ely, the area extends into Norfolk and Suffolk. The Black Fens commence a few miles north of Cambridge, and stretch out almost to Peterborough in the west and to beyond March in the north. On the eastern boundary there is a gradual transition into Breckland in the vicinity of Mildenhall and Lakenheath.

Fenland winter, Sixteen Foot Drain

A flat, almost hedgeless and treeless landscape is broken by 'islands' of higher ground on which towns and villages have been built. During the centuries of peat formation these areas of higher land, which protruded from the watery and swampy surroundings, provided the earliest settlers with firm land on which to build their dwellings, without the threat of flooding.

Many of the place names reflect 'island' origins by ending in 'ey' (Coveney, Stuntney, Thorney, Ramsey) or 'ea' (Manea, Eastrea, Stonea) which are derived from the Anglo-Saxon 'ig' meaning 'island'. Ely is thought to be derived from 'eel island' because of the enormous quantities of this fish which could be caught in nearby rivers and streams.

Ely's magnificent cathedral, founded in 673, dominates both city and surrounding fenland. It is a landmark visible from many miles away and there are especially good views from the Cambridge, Stuntney and Little Downham roads.

Rivers, also variously known as leams, drains, lodes, eaus and dykes, often run above the level of the surrounding land, and the extensive banks necessary to contain them are prominent features of the area. In some parts of the fens the 20-mile-long (32 kilometres) bank of the Hundred Foot Drain gives a distinct outline to the landscape. Since most of the rivers are artificial they are, in the main, straight and are often named after the persons who were instrumental in having them dug (Morton's Leam, Popham's Eau), or by their original width (Forty Foot Drain and Twenty Foot Drain).

In many places roads run alongside rivers. Sometimes the road is on a level with the top of the bank and is separated from the river by only a small bank (for example, the road alongside the Forty Foot Drain between Chatteris and Ramsey Forty Foot). In contrast, some roads run parallel to the river along the base of the bank which towers above (for example, the stretch of road between Earith and Sutton beside the Hundred Foot Drain). During the Second World War, to encourage agricultural production, concrete roads were laid on many of the peat tracks known as droves. These now serve as public roads and are usually single track with passing places. Comparison of maps printed prior to 1939 with recent editions shows what tremendous changes have taken place in the road system.

Access to many fen fields is still by droves which are usually wide enough to accommodate four lines of traffic. In most years by late autumn the droves are a morass of mud, passable only by farm tractors. In the summer they are often harrowed and rolled to level them off again. When the droves are dry any traffic creates a minor dust storm.

Construction of railways over fenland presented engineers with special and unusual problems. Vast quantities of ballast were required to provide foundations for the track. Over such a landscape cuttings are not necessary, but almost invariably where rail and road cross there is a level crossing or occasionally an underpass. Before the closure of some lines and the installation of automatic barriers on some of the remote lines, delays at level crossings had to be reckoned with in journeys across the fens.

The soil in the Black Fens is by no means universally black, although large areas of deep peat still remain near Littleport, Ely and Methwold, and in Holme Fen. Since drainage the peat has gradually wasted, causing a lowering of surface level, particularly on cultivated fields. Old river beds which have been exposed are now seen as ridges of silt meandering across the countryside. In many fields the peat has shrunk to such an extent that underlying subsoil is brought to the surface during ploughing, adding another hue to the soil. These different soils are seen most clearly in the spring, when they have dried out and have been cultivated for spring sowing.

In some areas (Soham Mere and Red Mere) soils are chalky white due to their formation by the precipitation of shell marl in freshwater lakes.

The dark soils give the fens a bleak and forlorn appearance during the winter, but in the spring a wide variety of crops clothe the flat land with many shades of green. Nowhere, except at sea, is there such an uninterrupted view of clouds and sky.

Formation and Early History of the Fens

Geology

In geological terms the Black Fens are recent, although the underlying clays, as for example, the Kimmeridge and Oxford, are very much older. Formation of the peat commenced about 8,000 years ago. Prior to this, during the Ice Ages, the British Isles were joined to the European continent, and the fenland rivers, the Welland, the Nene and the Ouse, were tributaries of the river Rhine. The rather unusual fish called barbot, which is said to be found only in rivers which were once joined to the Rhine, has occasionally been caught in fenland rivers.

During the Post-Glacial period sea levels rose throughout the planet. The level of the North Sea rose sufficiently to sever the British Isles from the rest of Europe, inundating the whole of the fenland area, and leaving only the islands of higher ground above the water. The subsequent development of peat and silt land has depended on the changes in relative levels of land and sea.

To seaward, silt was deposited by the rivers running into an enormous bay, the remnant of which today is called the Wash. These deposits accumulated gradually so that in periods when the sea level fell they formed a barrier, leaving a freshwater lake to landward. It was in the freshwater lake that peat formed, while the silt land gradually became more extensive. At first the silt land was the result of natural forces, but it has probably been extended since Roman times by the building of successive embankments to enclose saltings.

Peat is formed from the residue of plants growing in water or swampy conditions. When peat develops in a lake into which rivers are bringing silt and other soil particles it contains a certain amount of mineral matter, but when the lake is isolated from inflowing water the peat is almost entirely composed of decaying plant material.

When water is deep only aquatic plants survive, but the build-up of decaying leaves gradually reduces the

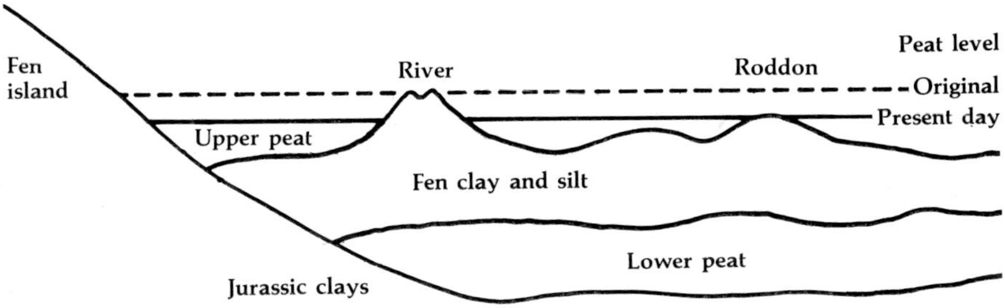

Section across the fens

depth until reeds can grow. As a reed swamp develops, water flow is impeded, causing deposition of any clay particles which it contains. Eventually the swamp becomes dry enough for other plants to grow, and if the process is allowed to continue for long enough, shrubs and trees will eventually begin to encroach upon the area. A miniature repetition of peat formation can be observed on the edge of lakes and ponds. If the water is shallow reed invasion is sometimes so aggressive that dredging is necessary to maintain an area of clear water.

The lower peat began to form towards the end of the Middle Stone Age (Mesolithic period) and continued through the New Stone Age (Neolithic period). At first it was formed only in the marginal waters but later it became much more general. During the lower peat phase there was some woodland, with oaks the predominant species.

This phase was followed by a marine transgression during which the fen clay was deposited. Fen clay is a very variable material and frequently contains a high proportion of silt. Because of its colour and consistency it is known locally as 'buttery blue' clay. This phase lasted until the early Bronze Age when the upper peat began to form.

While the upper peat was forming there was a period when the land was dry enough for trees, and the woods contained pine and yews in addition to oaks. Trunks from these trees are often ploughed out during farm cultivations, and in spite of the different species all are called 'bog oaks'. For an estimated 1,500 years formation of the upper peat continued, until the Romano-British period when there was another less extensive marine transgression during which the fenland meres were formed.

After this, peat formation continued over most of the Black Fens until the major drainage works were begun in the early 17th century.

The fens before drainage

Before drainage the Black Fens must have been bleak and forbidding, but for the early settlers they may have provided a refuge from warring tribes or an escape from the bondage of feudal England. Anyone who cared to venture into them could find enough dry land on which to build a primitive dwelling and a profusion of osiers, reeds and sedges with which to construct it. All the year round there was a superabundance of wild birds and fish to be had for the catching. For fuel, peat could be cut into turves during the summer and dried for winter use. For anyone who possessed domestic animals there was unlimited grazing in the low-lying fens during summer and enough higher ground on which to winter them.

The first inhabitants constructed round huts of wattle and mud daub with roofs of branches covered with reeds. A single opening in the roof let out the pungent smoke from the peat turves smouldering on a central hearth. Sedge provided a floor covering but cattle hides, sheep fleeces and feathers were used by some to add a few creature comforts to their humble lives. Until bricks and other materials became

Bog oaks, Holme Fen

readily available, fenmen relied on the natural products of this marshy region for building their homes.

Even in high summer the fens were difficult to cross on foot, and animals which strayed from the higher pastures might sink without trace into the boggy peat. In winter, when water was deeper, travelling by boat was possible unless the water was frozen, in which case pattens (skates) made from bones kept the inhabitants mobile. The fens have always been the mecca for long-distance skaters and many of the British speed-skating champions were born in the area.

Among the alders, willows, reeds and sedges which grew luxuriantly lived an unbelievably large number of species of birds. Some of these, now very rare, could be caught in sufficient numbers to be regarded as a normal part of the diet. It is said that during the 12th century it was easy to snare 'the crane, the heron, the wild duck, teal and most savoury snipe, the swallow-kite, the swarthy raven, the hoary vulture, the swift eagle, the greedy goshawk' and many others. It is difficult to identify with certainty all the birds mentioned, but it is probable that the swallow-kite is the red kite which is today just managing to survive in a few isolated areas of the Welsh mountains. Bird snaring in the fens continued for many centuries, and until 1920 larks were still being caught in this way for sale while plover netting ceased as recently as in 1947.

The muddy water also provided a bountiful supply of fish in great variety. Eels were especially valuable and were often supplied to religious establishments as payment for the right to use land or to fish in waters which they owned. At one time the Ramsey monks paid the monks of Peterborough 3,000 eels each Lent for the right to take stone from their quarry.

Even if the fens provided building materials and food in plenty they were by no means an idyllic place in which to live. In 1505 a traveller described them as 'a land of marshy ague and unwholesome swamps'. The early fenmen were tough and hardy but even they occasionally fell victim to malaria, rheumatism and other diseases in the general category of 'ague'. Specific remedies based on opium, or tea made from infusions of poppy seeds were sometimes used. It was said:

Poppy tea and opium pill
Are the fen cure for many an ill.

Inevitably there was belief in a number of folk cures, a common one being the wearing of eelskin garters to ward off rheumatism.

Although the natives acquired a degree of resistance to some of these diseases, they could prove fatal to newcomers. On one occasion when the Bishop of Ely presented the living of a fenland parish to a newcomer to the area, he did so on the condition that the rector would reside in another village on higher ground. He hoped that this would reduce the risk of the new incumbent's falling victim to ague through residing in the low-lying fenlands.

The history of the fens is reflected in the names given to the early natives by their highland neighbours: they were 'yellow bellies' because they lived a watery existence like frogs, and they were unkindly reported to have webbed feet; they were 'slodgers' because they splashed through the muddy water; and they were 'tigers' because of the ferocity with which they resisted early attempts to drain the fens.

The early settlers lived in harmony with their surroundings. They could almost subsist on what nature provided and could find enough dry land on which to grow some of the staple foods they required. Although they sought to preserve their fens they could not resist for ever the determined efforts of the drainers.

Drainage of the Fens

Some early attempts were made to improve drainage and thereby the agricultural value of the fens. The Romans constructed Car Dyke from near Cambridge to the north of Peterborough and beyond. This was mainly a canal for transporting food and other supplies from corn growing areas in the south to garrisons in the north, but it may also have served as a drain. A stretch of this old canal can be seen on the east side of the A10 road, near Waterbeach aerodrome.

Later, in about 1490, Bishop Morton dug a drain from Peterborough to Wisbech to improve drainage in the northern part of the Black Fens. His 'leam', which shortened the length of the river Nene, was an attempt to speed up the flow of the river and thereby reduce the silting which was tending to block the outfall below Wisbech.

In the early 17th century a group of 'Adventurers' led by the 4th Earl of Bedford, together with the Dutchman, Cornelius Vermuyden (later knighted for his drainage works), began drainage operations. The first major task was to dig the Old Bedford River, which was completed in 1630. It ran in a straight line from Earith to Denver, a distance of about 20 miles (32 kilometres), whereas the river Ouse followed a tortuous course through Ely of over 30 miles (48 kilometres). The new river was designed to take the water from the upper reaches in Bedfordshire and Huntingdonshire, thus relieving the Ely Ouse and making it better able to hold water from its various tributaries.

As a reward for financing drainage the Adventurers were to be allocated large tracts of fenland for their own use. After the completion of the Old Bedford River a Court held at St Ives in 1637 adjudged that drainage had been effectively carried out and each Adventurer was allotted his piece of land. A year later the decision was reversed on the grounds that although the Adventurers had improved the drainage, they had failed in the terms of the original agreement, as the area was still subject to flooding, especially in winter.

The 1637 adjudication was also unpopular as the commoners regarded it as an act of enclosure. King Charles I recognised this and in 1638 declared himself an undertaker, decreeing that even when land had been drained every man should remain in possession of his customary rights. He also formulated a grandiose scheme for a royal palace, Charlemont, to be built on the island where Manea now stands.

Oliver Cromwell, who was born in Huntingdon in 1599, and whose family had territorial possessions in the fens, was at the same time anxious to champion the commoners' cause. To delay the progress of the drainers he promulgated that 'Mr. Cromwell of Ely had undertaken, they the commoners paying him a groat for every cow they had upon the common, to hold the drainers in suit of law for five years and that in the meantime they should enjoy every part of their common'.

During the period from 1638 until the death of Charles I in 1649 there seems to have been no progress. Vermuyden could do no more than protect his previous work from the forces of

The sluice at Earith, with the Old Bedford River in the background

nature and from the activities of the 'Fen Tigers'. However, with the support of Oliver Cromwell, the Lord Protector, drainage work was eventually resumed in 1650 by the 5th Earl of Bedford, his father having died in 1641. Much of the digging was done by Scottish prisoners captured by Cromwell at the Battle of Dunbar, and later by Dutchmen taken prisoner during a naval engagement in the English Channel.

Vermuyden had spent the inactive years drawing up plans in preparation for the eventual resumption of work. In the early 1650s the Twenty Foot, Sixteen Foot and Forty Foot (also known as Vermuyden's) Drains were completed. The largest and most important task, however, was to dig the Hundred Foot Drain or New Bedford River. This was another attempt to reduce the risk of flooding from the river Ouse. To do this, an area of about 5,000 acres (2,000 hectares), known as the Hundred Foot Washes, between the two rivers was to be used as a plain where flood water could be held safely until river levels fell sufficiently for the water to be discharged at Wellmore Lake Sluice.

Flooding of the Ouse Washes, as this area is now called, is controlled by operation of sluice gates at Earith. Normally, water from the river Ouse flows down the Hundred Foot Drain, which is tidal throughout its length. When the river at Earith reaches flood level, sluice gates at the head of the Old Bedford are opened. This river has a high bank on its northwest, or outer side, but as there is scarcely a bank on its inner side, water overflows into the Washes. Eventually it is discharged back into the Hundred Foot Drain from the river Delph through Wellmore Lake Sluice.

The Old Bedford River is within the Washes as far as Welches Dam where the Forty Foot Drain originally emptied into it. From this point to Denver the Old Bedford is on the north of the bank and the river Delph has been dug to connect with Wellmore Lake Sluice.

Only three roads cross the Washes. The most frequently flooded is at Sutton Gault where there is an elevated pathway for pedestrians. At Mepal there is a causeway which is above flood level, but the road further north at Welney is subject to occasional flooding, although it is usually passable by vehicles with high ground clearance.

Over the centuries modifications have been made to both sluices and outfalls, but Vermuyden's drains still remain as an impressive monument to his skill and perseverance. Some idea of the magnitude of his task can be gained when it is remembered that all the work over this swampy land had to be carried out with only shovels, wheelbarrows and horses against the harassment of the natives and endless financial anxiety. Vermuyden's engineers must have worked with great tenacity and dedication to complete this colossal undertaking.

When planning drainage of the fens Vermuyden overlooked the vital fact that when the peat began to dry it would waste and shrink. Soon land levels fell, and when rivers overflowed their banks disastrous floods were inevitable. A few years after the completion of the main rivers there was widespread flooding with 'corn stacks three feet [1 metre] deep in water' in some areas. Periodic inundations, or 'drownings' as they were called, have occurred ever since, causing great privation and sometimes ruination to farmers.

A contemporary account of the 'great drowned' of 1796 describes how the news was received: 'It was Saturday the bank broke and about the middle of the day but it was some way from us and it was late in the afternoon when a man on horseback came round to our farm calling out "The bank's

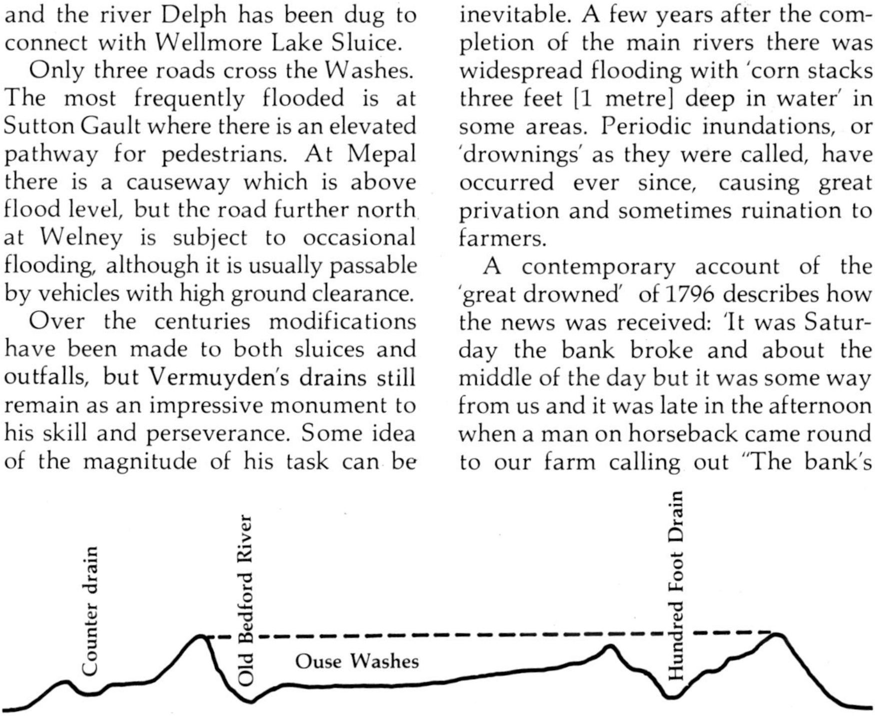

Section of the Washes south of Welches Dam

broke, the bank's broke." Then he went round to our neighbours and everybody knew what THAT meant and began getting their cattle together and moving them to a place of safety before the water was on them.'

After working through the night the farmer managed to get his corn ready for loading the next morning and, together with the cattle, reached the higher land at Littleport before flood water overtook him. For ten days the family was marooned and 'lived upstairs as the lower rooms were full'. Eventually they were rescued and after a time returned to their 'little house and became settled once more. Still it was an anxious time for the land was under water all that summer and we could sow no crops. So when wheat was a guinea a bushel [4 pence a kilogramme] we had none to sell but had to buy flour at seven shillings a stone [5½ pence a kilogramme] for our own use.'

This family was fortunate, however, as many of their friends lost everything, and four out of the five nearby farmers 'never farmed again but had to take to day labour for a living'. Conditions continued to deteriorate, and in 1805, after a visit to the fens, Arthur Young wrote: 'In the last 30 years many inundations have taken place. The remedies that have been applied by numberless Acts of Parliament have been in vain, but the burden by taxes immense.'

There are two main reasons why cutting new rivers and straightening existing courses failed to prevent flooding. First, the fenland rivers have very little natural fall and therefore tend to run sluggishly. Silt in river beds and outfalls accumulates at an alarming rate. The situation is made worse by the incursion of salt water heavily laden with silt which comes in with high tides from the Wash. Flow of fresh water on the ebbing tide is inadequate to remove silt deposited when the tide turns, and thus there is a tendency for estuaries to become silted up which further reduces the rate of discharge of river water.

Second, as a result of peat shrinkage which followed drainage, rivers were gradually left above land level. It was not possible to lower river levels because all the outfalls were through stable silt lands and the only way to contain the water was to embank.

Wherever possible, clay for embanking was dug nearby, but where local material was unsuitable or covered by too great a depth of peat, clay had to be brought up by barge. Although known locally as gault, most of the material used was Kimmeridge clay, obtained from Roswell Pits, Ely.

The pits can be seen by following the nature trail designed by the Cambridgeshire and Isle of Ely Naturalists' Trust, which starts in Springhead Lane, Ely. Guides can be purchased in some local shops. The pits are now used for sailing by the Ely Sailing Club.

Before the coming of machines, men engaged on loading the barges by hand were termed 'gaulters' and those who made the banks were known as 'bankers'. There is a story of an incredulous visiting judge being confronted by one of these workmen still dressed in his muddy attire who, on being asked, 'What is your work?', replied, 'I am a banker.'

As soon as it became necessary to embank the main rivers a method had to be devised by which water from the lower lying field drains could be raised into them. One of the earliest records of a windmill used for drainage in the fens was at Over in 1604, even before the major drainage work had commenced.

Windmills subsequently became a feature of the fenland scene. They were used to drive scoop-wheels which were probably introduced to the fens by Dutch engineers. These wheels, which have paddles set at an angle of about 30 degrees, were made to rotate in a channel cut in the peat. As they turned, water was temporarily trapped by each paddle before running out. By virtue of the speed of rotation water can be lifted effectively in this way to about one-fifth of the wheel's diameter.

The windmills were built of wood on foundations of piles driven through the soft peat to the firmer clay below. The first scoop-wheels were also made entirely of wood but later the centres were made of cast iron. Even then, oak or fir paddles were still used. For more efficient operation the channels were lined with bricks, because, when made of peat only, they tended to become too wide and water escaped and ran back into the field drain.

The only surviving drainage windmill in the fens is at Wicken. It had to be restored extensively when it was moved from Adventurers Fen where it was known as Norman's Mill and was used until the early 1930s. The scoop-wheel is now used occasionally to lift water into Wicken Fen to maintain a high water level for conservation purposes.

Vancouver, in 1794, described travelling along the road built on the bank of the Forty Foot Drain between Chatteris and Ramsey Forty Foot: '... even in summer when the carriage path is pretty good there is some little cause of alarm to the mere *terra-firma* traveller. In winter, when the drainage windmills are at work close to the road (their business being to throw the water out of a minor catch water drain, on one side of the road, into the main drain on the other – through tunnels beneath it) the foaming currents gushing out in full view – it would seem to be almost a miracle that a carriage drawn by startling horses not used to such a sight should escape harm.'

When wind was the motive power, 25 feet (7.6 metres) was the practical maximum diameter for scoop-wheels. Although wheels of this size could lift water 5 feet (1.5 metres) they worked

Action of scoop-wheel

more efficiently when a lift of no more than 3 feet (1 metre) was required. As the peat shrank, lifts greater than 5 feet (1.5 metres) became necessary and then two windmills had to be used to raise the water in stages. Eventually, in some places, a series of windmills had to be installed to get rid of water from very low-lying areas.

Wind is notoriously unreliable, and too often as water levels in field drains rose steadily the mills stood idle or worked inefficiently due to lack of wind. The inadequacy of this system led to many serious floods, and an alternative source of power had to be sought.

To overcome the problem steam engines began to be used, the first being installed at Sutton St Edmunds in about 1817. Although it had a comparatively short life, being scrapped in 1834, it was the forerunner of many others, some of which worked for almost one hundred years before being replaced by diesel engines.

The increased power provided by steam enabled much larger scoop-wheels to be used. The largest, which was fitted to the Hundred Foot engine in 1881, had a diameter of 50 feet (152 metres), had 60 paddles and weighed 75 tons (76 tonnes).

A plaque on the outside of the building commemorates the part played by steam in fen drainage:

These FENS have oft times been by
WATER drowned,
Science a remedy in WATER found.
The power of STEAM she said shall
be employ'd
And the destroyer by itself destroy'd.

Another plaque on the same building records the changes which have taken place:

1756 Windmill
1830 80 h.p. steam engine
1882 Power increased to about 224 h.p. by improved valve gear and increased boiler pressure
1914 400 h.p. Gwynnes steam engine and pump replaced scoop wheel, discharge 200 tons per minute
1926 230 h.p. Mirrlees oil engine in a separate house in addition to Gwynnes set
1951 540 h.p. Ruston oil engine replaces Gwynnes set

In addition to scoop-wheels, pumps of various types were used, the most notable being the Appold centrifugal pump which was used to drain Whittlesey Mere in 1852. It was the largest made at that time and had previously been shown at the Great Exhibition in London in 1851. An impeller from this pump is preserved in the Science Museum in South Kensington, London.

The new pump, and the fact that Whittlesey was the last mere to be drained, attracted large crowds of sightseers, most of whom came prepared with sacks and baskets to take home fish which could be caught easily as they floundered in the shallow waters. A few of the more enterprising visitors came with carts so that they could gather enough fish to send to markets in London and the Midlands. The largest fish caught was the legendary 'great pike of Whittlesey Mere' which, although it was said to be old, nevertheless weighed 52 lb (24 kilogrammes). Drainage of the mere exposed some large, roughly cut pieces of stone thought to have been destined for Ramsey Abbey before the small craft in which they were being carried sank in a storm. Also found were a silver incense boat, a silver censer and silver chandelier (now in the Victoria and Albert Museum in London), all of which have been identified as originating from Ramsey Abbey.

Drainage of Whittlesey Mere could be undertaken only because of the improvements made to the Middle Level drainage system between 1844 and 1848. The major part of the scheme was the extension of the Sixteen Foot Drain in a northerly direction for a distance of 10 miles (16 kilometres). This involved cutting under Well Creek at Outwell, thus creating the only aqueduct in the fens. The outfall of this new channel, which is called the Middle Level Main Drain, is at Wiggenhall St Germans, where the tidal level is 8 feet (2.5 metres) lower than at the original sluice at Salters Lode. Thus water which formerly flowed into the Forty Foot Drain and then to the Old Bedford River at Welches Dam was directed to Wiggenhall St Germans.

Gravity drainage only was in operation until the 1930s when it became inadequate for the discharge of water from the ever shrinking fens. Between 1930 and 1934 a pumping station was constructed and three 1,000 h.p. diesel driven pumps were installed.

By 1951 gravity drainage could no longer be used and a further pump was installed so that all the water from the Middle Level could be pumped into the Ouse. Pumping capacity was increased in 1970 and the station is now able to discharge 3,990 tons (4,053 tonnes) or almost one million gallons (4.5 million litres) per minute against the worst tidal period.

Over the last few years further improvements have been made to the drains, many of them having been widened and deepened. Often, as for instance on the Sixteen Foot Drain, this has necessitated rebuilding most of the bridges.

The whole region of the fens is divided for drainage purposes into Internal Drainage Board areas. Each is responsible for a certain area and controls the pumps which lift water into the main drains. During the last two decades most of the small diesel pumps have been replaced by automatic electric pumps, but in the larger stations many diesels are still retained alongside new electric pumps, as stand-by units.

A remarkable combination of circumstances occurred in early 1947 to cause one of the worst floods ever recorded in the fens and, indeed, over the whole of the British Isles. The rainfall in 1946 had been exceptionally high and was followed by heavy snow and rainfall which resulted in the equivalent of over 12 inches (30 centimetres) of rain in the first three months of 1947.

In March the onset of the thaw was accompanied by heavy rain but the land was still in the iron grip of frost, which forced the rain to run off into rivers and ditches. Rivers soon began to rise rapidly as ice floes restricted normal flow. In the fens ice blocked rivers and drains, and pumps could not work at full capacity simply because water was not flowing quickly enough to them. The exceptionally hard frosts had penetrated the clay banks which were thus weakened and unable to withstand the abnormal stress to which they were subjected. Serious breaches occurred in the banks of the Wissey, Little Ouse and Old West Rivers, causing widespread flooding and extensive damage. Some of the land in Hilgay Fen was covered by 15 feet (4.5 metres) of water, and at Southery the force of the water completely destroyed one house which stood in its path.

A full emergency relief operation was soon started: army amphibious tanks were sent to close breaches, Dutch cranes were used to rebuild banks, and hundreds of pumps were collected from all over the country and from The Netherlands to attempt to dispose of the flood water.

Recovery was sufficiently fast for most of the fens to be sown with crops in the spring, although many had to be sown late. The main exception was in Haddenham Fen where, because the land level is so low, it was not until July that the pumps finished working.

These extensive floods demonstrated the vulnerability of the eastern part of the Black Fens to flooding. Water in the rivers, which is 6 feet (1.8 metres) above land level in normal times, can under flood conditions rise to twice this level. Further embanking or widening was not considered to be a satisfactory solution to the problem, but, instead, a flood protection scheme costing

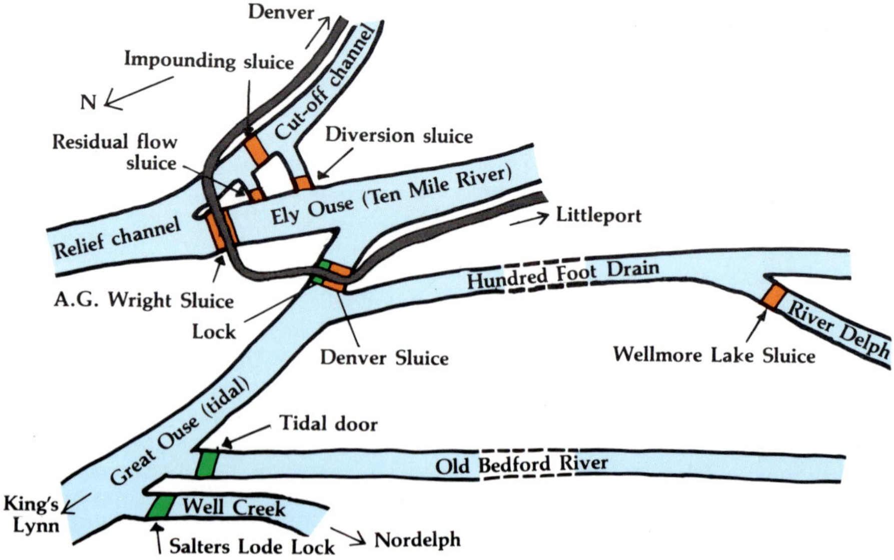

Denver Sluice

Denver Sluice and Lock (*left*) and A.G. Wright Sluice (*right*)

£11 million was completed in 1964. This involved cutting a new relief channel 11 miles (17.5 kilometres) long from Denver to King's Lynn and the construction of a new sluice at Denver to allow water from the Ely Ouse (or Ten Mile River) to be discharged into it.

The scheme also involved digging a cut-off channel 27 miles (43 kilometres) long from near Mildenhall to Denver. This runs round the edge of the fens, and water from the Lark, Little Ouse and Wissey can be diverted into it. In times of flood about 40 per cent of the water which would otherwise have been carried by the Ely Ouse can be diverted directly to Denver. It is interesting to note that the cut-off channel follows very closely the line along which Vermuyden had suggested the digging of a drain.

For over three hundred years the only water control function at Denver was to discharge water as quickly as possible, but since 1971 it has been possible to direct water from the Ely Ouse to Essex. This is achieved by reversing the flow on the cut-off channel by directing water from the Ouse into it at Denver. At Blackdyke intake it passes into a tunnel of approximately 8 feet (2.5 metres) in diameter driven through gault clay to Kennett pumping station. Here it is lifted into a pipeline which discharges it into the headwaters of the river Stour, down which it can flow to Stratford St Mary and thence be pumped into Abberton Reservoir. A pipeline from Wixoe to the river Colne and river Pant allows water to be diverted down these rivers to service the Ardleigh and Hanningfield Reservoirs.

The Fens since Drainage

Economic activities

In their undrained state most of the low-lying fens were used either for summer grazing or left untended to produce reeds, sedge or willows. Much of the area was probably scrub of alder and blackthorn which was left in its wild state. On completion of the major drainage work in the late 17th century, more land was available for growing arable crops as it was considered to be safe from flooding throughout the year.

Crops included oats, wheat, rye and coleseed. The oats were used chiefly for animals, as was the coleseed; the wheat and rye were ground into flour. Bringing tufted rough pasture into arable cultivation must have been difficult with the horse-drawn implements available at the time. To get rid of matted growth and roots, a practice which involved ploughing about 2 inches (5 centimetres) deep was followed by the collection of the disturbed vegetation and peat into heaps, which were then burned. This was termed 'paring and burning' and was the usual practice before sowing coleseed.

At first the coleseed or rape (now usually called oilseed rape) was used mainly for grazing sheep which constituted much of the farming economy at that time. By the beginning of the 19th century the seed of coleseed was in considerable demand for crushing for the production of colza oil for use in lamps. The light given by oil lamps was superior to that of the traditional candles or rushlights (rush stems dipped in tallow).

For burning in lamps colza oil competed with whale oil and eventually virtually replaced it. Its production became an important industry in the fens but it finally died out when mineral oils became available. At one time there were seven oil crushing mills in Wisbech alone and 'no less than 9,000 acres [3,600 hectares] of the Great Beford Level, equal to one-thirteenth of its entire extent, carried every year a crop of rape for seed'. Colza oil lamps were widely used by railway companies, and in 1850 the North Western alone required an annual supply of 40,000 gallons (180,000 litres), which probably represented the produce from at least 600 acres (240 hectares).

Hemp was another unusual crop, formerly widely grown in the fens, as the soils which suited it best were those with a high organic matter content, with plenty of moisture. This vigorously growing plant, which attained a height of 6 feet (1.8 metres), was able to suppress the profuse weed growth found in fenland soils. The long stems yielded fibres from which the ropes needed for sailing ships could be made. It is probable that the fenmen recognised 'pot' in the seed which they smoked. Workers were said to become drowsy after working for long hours in the crop or in the 'factories' where seed was threshed out and the fibres prepared for retting.

In spite of land drainage, intensive use of the fens for farming was able to develop only very slowly because of poor accessibility. Isolated hamlets grew up along some of the main rivers, with water traffic the chief means of transport. By land, the approach to the

Barges carrying clay for repairs to river banks

hamlet might have been one or two miles of soft peat drove to the hard public road. Such roads could be used by horse and cart for part of the year but in winter they became impassable.

It was inevitable that barge traffic developed to serve the needs of these hamlets and also to move produce out of the fens. During the 18th century cargoes coming into the fens through Denver lock included coal, salt, timber, iron and pitch. These could be delivered to the hythes or small quays possessed by many of the villages, and there was access along the Ouse up to Bedford, on the Cam up to Cambridge and through the man-made lodes to places such as Swaffham Bulbeck and Reach. The rivers Wissey, Little Ouse and Lark were also navigable well into Norfolk and Suffolk.

Home produce, including wheat, oats, rye and coleseed, could be moved from farm quay to mills in the area or to King's Lynn for transhipping.

With the coming of steam tugs the fenland barge traffic increased, making possible further expansion of crop production. Soon after the introduction of railways, tracks were constructed across the fens. In addition to providing loading facilities at stations, railway companies made sidings where farm produce could be loaded and coal and fertiliser brought in.

At Ely, Littleport and Benwick, quays were made in the station yard so that farm barges could be readily unloaded into railway waggons. Commercial traffic has now ceased, but the waterways are used by a considerable number of pleasure and holiday craft.

Borough Fen Decoy, with pipe, reed screens and dog leaps

Wildlife

Drainage did not have the immediate and dramatic effect on wildlife that many of the natives feared. There were still a number of swampy areas frequented by wildfowl, and fish remained plentiful in the numerous drains and meres. To some extent the lot of the wildfowler was improved, as it became possible to construct and operate large duck decoys once the water levels were no longer subject to large and unpredictable changes.

One of the earliest recorded decoys is at Borough Fen, near Peterborough, which was probably established about 1670 (see Cook and Pilcher, *The History of Borough Fen Decoy*, Providence Press 1982). The decoys consisted of a number of netted channels, or pipes, evenly spaced round a pond. One side of the pipe had small screens of wattle or reeds placed in a zig-zag manner, with a low connecting screen over which the decoyman's dog (usually called 'Piper', and fox-like in appearance) was trained to leap. From the entrance the pipe decreased gradually in size to a 'tunnel' or 'purse' into which the ducks were eventually driven and caught. Live decoy ducks were sometimes kept on the pond to entice migratory wild ducks to come down. The pipe selected for use on any one day was the one into which the wind was blowing directly, to ensure that the ducks did not scent the decoyman. Some operators carried a smouldering peat turf to mask their scent by another with which the ducks would be familiar.

To entice the ducks into the pipe some grain was put near the entrance. The decoyman was able to peep through the reed screens and as soon as the ducks were near enough he set his dog to work. The dog would leap over one of the small screens, run alongside one of the large screens in full view of the ducks, until he jumped back over another small screen to disappear. The process, under the control of the decoyman, might be repeated a few times until the ducks were attracted by the sudden appearance and disappearance of the dog. When their curiosity had been aroused they would swim towards the point where the dog last disappeared.

The dog would then be sent round each hurdle in succession until the ducks were well into the pipe. The decoyman would suddenly appear at the entrance to the pipe and the frightened birds would swim or fly into the narrow end where they were trapped and killed for market. Killing of ducks at Borough Fen ceased in 1954 and since then the decoy has been used exclusively for ringing purposes by the Wildfowl Trust.

Another method used for killing large numbers of wildfowl was punt gunning. A very large gun was fixed to a small punt which was propelled forward slowly by the gunner lying prone. With small poles, or punts, or just with his hands in the icy water, he

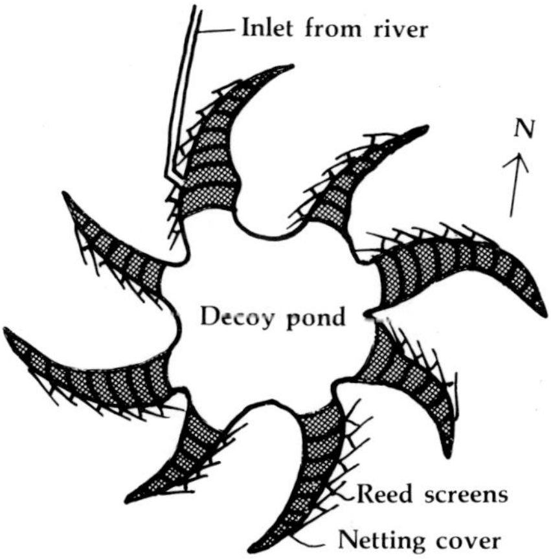

Eight-pipe decoy, Borough Fen

would, as quickly as possible, stalk rafts of ducks feeding in the shallow water of a flooded marsh or on open water until they were in range. A single shot from one of these mighty guns might kill 10, 20 or even 30 birds. The wounded ducks were rounded up and added to the gunner's bag. Punt guns were last used in the fens on the flooded Ouse Washes but the practice had ceased by the end of the 1960s.

Dry areas within flooded marshes were used for netting plovers until this practice was banned in 1947. Decoy plovers and imitation calls made on a reed whistle enticed the birds down into a small area. The catcher was then able to release his pre-set spring-loaded net over the flock. Large numbers were caught in this way and sent to market by the sackful for sale for a few pence each (see G.H. (Josh) Scott, *From Guns to Binoculars*, Providence Press 1980).

In the Middle Ages large tracts of undrained fens were used for rearing flocks of geese, which provided both food and quill feathers. In the early 19th century it was customary to pluck for quills four times during the year. Usually, ten feathers were taken from each goose on each occasion, the value being about 6d (2½ pence) per 100. In spite of the huge number of geese kept, there was such a demand for quills that some had to be imported. In 1854 it was estimated that 'We imported upwards of 12 millions and a half of goose and swan quills valued at £10,282.'

One fen farmer at about this time had 160 breeding stock, and from them he expected to rear in a good year 700, and in a bad year 500. Then, as now, prices were unpredictable and liable to violent fluctuations: the farmer said that he had previously sold each for 1 shilling (5 pence), and yet that year each was selling for 2 shillings (10 pence), which was higher than ever. As his expense for corn was not very great (£20 in a mild winter and up to £50 in a severe one) he could make a profit of about £40 from his flock. This enterprise had the added advantage that his wife and children could attend to the geese.

As there were tens of thousands of geese produced in the fens, most of them had to be sent a considerable distance to market. Many went to London, doing the journey on foot, in large droves. Before starting their walk it was customary, in some parts of the country, to prepare the birds' feet by driving them two or three times through a compound of tar, sawdust and sand. This produced a pad on their webbed feet which eventually fell off leaving a clean skin. In *A Tour through England and Wales* (1724-7) Daniel Defoe describes how: 'A prodigious number of geese are brought up to London in droves from the farthest part of Norfolk, even from the fenn-country, about Lynn, Downham, Wisbech and the Washes ... 'tis very frequent now to meet droves with a thousand, sometimes two thousand in a drove. They begin to drive them generally in August by which time the harvest is almost over and the geese may feed in the stubble as they go. Thus they hold on to the end of October when the roads begin to be too stiff and deep for their broad feet and short leggs to march in.'

Even after drainage fish could still be netted in large enough quantities to supply the increasing demands of towns. But they could be sold only if they were kept alive during the long and slow journey to market. In 1724 Defoe described how he saw fish being caught in the fens and being carried to London in waggons loaded with butts: 'The buts have a little square flap instead of a bung, about 10, 12 or 14 inches [25 to 35 centimetres] square, which being open'd gives air to the fish and every night when they come to the inn, they draw off the water and let more fresh and sweet water run into them again. In these carriages they chiefly carry tench and pike, pearch and eels, but especially tench and pike of which here are some of the largest in England.'

Eels could be caught singly using a pronged glaive on a long shaft. It was pushed into the mud and the eels became impaled on its barbed prongs. For catching large numbers of eels, traps made from osiers were used, while fish were usually caught by netting the narrow rivers and streams.

A few eels for sale are still caught in basket traps. The fenland rivers provide fine sport for enthusiastic anglers who come from far and wide to try their luck in the hope of landing a really large pike.

Turf cutting

Formerly, most parishes had a common or turf fen where peat could be cut for fuel. The usual practice was to cut sufficient turves for a winter's supply as soon as the land was reasonably dry in spring. A special triangular-shaped spade was used for clearing the rough sedge and weeds, and then the turves were cut with a becket. They would be stacked and left to dry out during the summer, and then carted home on a turf barrow which was similar to a wheelbarrow, without legs.

The size of turves varied from parish to parish. At Isleham, for instance, they were 2.5 inches (6.5 centimetres) square and 18 to 20 inches (45 to 50 centimetres) long. At Wicken they were nearly twice as big as this when freshly cut, but when dried shrank to about 4 inches (10 centimetres) by 3 inches (8 centimetres) by 10 inches (25 centimetres).

Some peat cutters earned a living by selling their turves in Cambridge. In the early 19th century Isleham turves fetched 8 shillings (40 pence) a thousand, and land from which turf could be cut was valued at from £50 to £80 per acre (£125 to £200 per hectare). There is an account from this period of a man who cut turves at Isleham. For transportation he used a home-made barge which he pulled himself. The journey to Cambridge must have been more than 30 miles (48 kilometres), and at one point the barge had to be unloaded, pulled across a road, and then reloaded before the journey could be resumed. He often did this journey twice each week.

Although turf cutting has ceased, peat fires started unintentionally are by no means uncommon. In summer, when something is being burned, the peat will ignite if dry, and will smoulder to form a pit if not dealt with promptly. Once alight it is not easy to extinguish, and in some years local fire brigades are kept very busy. Water alone is not usually sufficient to quench the burning peats, the most effective method being to dig around the pit and dampen it well. The reddish-brown ashes which remain can be seen clearly during subsequent cultivation.

The shrinking peat

In an undrained state fen soil may contain up to 95 per cent water and only 5 per cent peat. Drainage has the immediate effect of removing most of the water in the upper layers, causing a consequent drop in land level. When dry, it oxidises, which causes further wastage. Under arable cropping, where land is ploughed and cultivated,

Peat burning, Waterden Fen, Ely

wastage can be from a half to one inch (one to two centimetres) per year or, as the farmer says: 'Peat shrinks the height of a man in the life of a man'.

A measure of the rate of shrinkage can be obtained from Holme Post in Denton Fen, Holme, on the edge of the former Whittlesey Mere. The top of this post, which may have come from the Great Exhibition building of 1851, is at the original level of the land. In the first 30 years there was a very rapid shrinkage of peat and the land level dropped by over 8 feet (2.4 metres). In the following hundred years to 1981, there was a further loss of 4 feet (1.2 metres); the decrease in shrinkage rate may be attributed to the fact that since about 1917 the post has been surrounded by birch woodland which has protected the peat from rapid wastage. When Holme Post became unstable in the 1950s, another post was erected nearby on a concrete base to ensure that the levels were faithfully recorded while the old post was being restored.

Over the centuries since drainage was first undertaken shrinkage has gradually led to the exposure and admixture of subsoil with the peat. This process occurred first on the marginal areas where the peat was thinnest, and thus peat soil, which has a high mineral content, is called skirtland. Such skirt soils are now widespread but some areas of deep peat soils still remain.

The drop in land level as a result of peat wastage has had a marked effect on the fenland landscape. While existing rivers which flow above ground level have had to be embanked, the former courses of extinct rivers have become exposed as silty hillocks, known as roddons or rodhams.

During peat formation rivers flowed from the surrounding highlands, carrying large quantities of silt. When their flow was impeded across the flat fenland much of the carried material was deposited on the river bed. Accumulation of silt went on for centuries until there was a change in water level and the whole of the fenland basin was inundated. The river beds became covered with a peat deposit, so that when the area was first drained no visual evidence of the former rivers remained. Shrinkage of the peat has exposed them as small hills winding across the countryside.

One of the largest is the bed of the former course of the Little Ouse which is clearly visible between Littleport and Kenney Hill near Mildenhall. At the Littleport end the roddon can be seen to cross and recross the road but the road has, in recent years, been levelled where it cuts through. Advantage was taken of the firm base that the roddon provided, and a number of houses have been built along it.

Some roads have been constructed on roddons as, for example, between Chatteris and Somersham. At Prickwillow the main street is on the roddon of the extinct course of the Ely Ouse. Houses have been built off the roddon and most are well below road level. Benwick is another example of a village with the main street on a roddon. Some of the houses were built with their foundations partly on the silt and partly on peat. As a result of peat shrinkage the foundations at the rear have fallen and the houses now lean back, away from the street. On some houses the doors and windows have been rehung, giving the front walls a buttress-like appearance.

Few of the older cottages and buildings on the peat are now upright because of the poor unstable base which the peat provided. When the peat was very deep cottages had to be constructed on a raft principle. Usually walls were supported on trunks or planks of wood, but floors were laid on the flattened peat. The wood seemed to be preserved by the peat and persisted for many years, but settling occurred due to compression by the weight of the building and due to peat wastage.

Settling was very seldom uniform and most old cottages built on the raft principle now have a lean in one direction or another. Usually the added strength of a chimney breast was sufficient to hold the centre or an end wall upright. On some double dwellings with a chimney at each end there was a tendency for the centre to settle giving the house a broken back appearance. If the walls sank faster than the floor then more earth was dug out to maintain sufficient headroom. With uneven floors it was necessary to support furniture with wedges.

Modern construction methods using reinforced concrete rafts are usually successful, but even these are not always sufficiently strong to prevent deep cracks developing in walls.

More stable foundations were provided for some buildings by making use of the firmer subsoil clay. This was done either by driving piles into the clay or by digging down and building up from the clay. The signal box at Black Bank, Little Downham, is a good example of the pile method. Although it originally stood at ground level it is now well above the surrounding fields and peat wastage has exposed the piles.

The second method, that of building up from the clay, was rather like building a cellar, the walls of which gradually became uncovered. As the peat has shrunk from around these houses extra steps have had to be added to reach doors. At Prickwillow Vicarage there are now nine steps where there were only two when it was built. The clear line of the original ground level can be seen on many buildings and there are numerous examples of similar adjustments to steps throughout the Black Fens. Some householders have given up the struggle to maintain access to certain doors which they have bricked up and abandoned.

Roads frequently run alongside river courses, probably because the silt and clay banks made better foundations than peat alone. Since peat below the road is not exposed to the atmosphere it wastes only very slowly, and consequently many roads are now slightly elevated above the surrounding farmland. Wastage at the exposed edges is rather greater, which is the cause of subsidence to road surfaces. To overcome this problem on more important roads banks of earth are made alongside.

During the feverish expansion of railways in the mid 19th century the fenland town of March became a major marshalling yard as it was strategically placed between networks in the east, the Midlands and the north. Here there was a sufficient area of mineral soil to build up a complex of sidings, engine sheds and shunting facilities, but the construction of tracks from Ely, Peterborough and elsewhere was difficult and expensive.

Many devices had to be used to make a sufficiently firm foundation for the track. Where the peat was still wet and boggy as, for instance, near rivers, large quantities of brushwood, sand and hardcore disappeared into the quagmire before a satisfactory causeway began to form. All bridges had to be built on piles, as did any signal boxes or other essential buildings. As far as possible stations were constructed on islands of mineral soil to avoid construction difficulties.

Soon after completion of the tracks, peat shrinkage became a problem. The weight of ballast and heavy locomotives caused some lowering of the track through compaction, added to which was the gradual peat wastage. Tracks which ran from island to island, often crossing roddons in their path, required frequent additions of fresh ballast to

House (now abandoned) with doors well above ground level due to peat shrinkage, Thorney

maintain them at their original level.

One notable effect of the drainage of Whittlesey Mere was the increase in the annual rate of subsidence of the railway line running from Holme to Peterborough. In the first years after drainage the line, which was already 4 feet (1.2 metres) above ground level, required seven times as much ballast as would normally have been used each year, to make good the extra wastage.

Addition of ballast has, in effect, built up embankments, so that all railway lines across the fens are well above ground level. Many old drain culverts under railways are now too high to be effective, and either they have had to be lowered at considerable expense, or new drains have been dug to take away water by another route. Approach roads to level crossings now slope up to the line whereas originally they were level with it. Peat still underlies both roads and railways, a fact which is very obvious when a train thunders over a level crossing causing the road to vibrate for a short distance on both sides of the line.

Bog oaks

During the development of the fens, large areas were covered once or twice with forests. When the land was flooded and conditions became unfavourable, the trees died and fell into the swampy water in which peat was forming. The trunks have been preserved in the peat, and a number lie just above the mineral subsoil. Gradually, as a result of peat shrinkage, many have become exposed during farming operations.

At first only small branches are uncovered, but in later years the trunks are struck by implement tines and have to be removed. The smaller trunks can be pulled out with a farm tractor but some are so large that even with a bulldozer they can be difficult to unearth and remove.

When large numbers of bog oaks are found some farmers will make huge heaps in their fields. These will be left to dry out for a year or two before being burned. The more usual procedure is to leave them on roadside verges until they are dry enough to burn. They are often used for firewood, but in the wet state can be difficult to cut because the wood fibres are stringy and saws do not work smoothly through them. On the other hand, if they are left to dry for too long they become so hard that it is almost impossible to make any impact on them.

Fen blows

In the spring, when much of the land is bare, the light and friable peat is easily picked up by the gale force winds which sweep across the open countryside. At first only a low dusty fog is formed, but as the wind strengthens large dust clouds billowing into the air can be seen for a considerable distance. The dust can become dense enough to obscure sunlight, and driving in a 'blow' is similar to being in a really thick smog except that there is the added hazard of dust penetrating even the smallest opening.

Great inconvenience is experienced by householders living in the path of a blow. The peat dust drifts like powder around doorways and windows and infiltrates every nook and cranny.

Blows may, however, be only a few yards wide as they originate from a field or part of a field where soil conditions are dry enough for the wind to lift the peat.

When blows occur just after crops have been drilled, seed and fertiliser are swept away either on to another field or into a fieldside dyke. If there are young seedlings during a blow the abrasive particles of dust will shred the tender leaves, and if the blow is prolonged soil is blown away, exposing roots and even dislodging entire plants.

Loss of yield because of damage to plants, together with the cost of resowing, can be serious. There is the added expense of clearing dykes which have been filled with peat, an operation which has to be carried out immediately in case heavy rain should follow and fields become waterlogged because of impeded drainage.

Peat to which clay or silt has been added is much more resistant to blowing. In the last century and well into the

Fen blow, Manea Road, Wimblington

present, it was customary in the fens to 'clay' land in places where there were about 4 to 5 feet (1.2 to 1.5 metres) of peat. The aim was to dig clay from below the peat and spread it over the surface. Trenches were dug across the fields and after the peat had been removed, about 2 feet (0.6 metre) of clay was dug out and the trench filled with peat. While working in the trench the workman could not be seen; the only signs that he was there were the spadefuls of clay being thrown up.

The effect of spreading quite a small amount of clay was beneficial for 20 years or more, after which a further claying might be undertaken. In dry years the course of a clay dyke can be traced on many fields by the better growth above it. When new drains are cut the remains of clay dykes are sometimes exposed as a row of rec-

Straw planted to prevent blowing, near Littleport

tangles of peat within the clay.

Various methods are used today to reduce the risk of damage from blows. Sometimes faster growing plants, such as mustard or barley, are sown between the rows of slower growing crops such as sugar beet and onions. When the crop is well enough established to withstand a blow, the nurse crop is killed off with a selective weedkiller.

In some areas straw is planted to prevent blowing in the spring. A machine, which has a conveyor belt down which the straw travels until it is pressed into the ground with a disc coulter, is used to plant rows of straw between crop rows. During the summer the straw gradually disintegrates and causes no problems when the beet or onions are harvested.

Agriculture

The highly fertile peat soils of the fens are now some of the most productive in Britain, and the whole area is devoted to intensive agricultural and horticultural crops. Some of the less fertile land on the fen islands remains in grass which is used for dairy and beef cattle. The only other expanse of grass in the Black Fens is in the Washes.

Farms vary enormously in size: many are only a few acres in extent and are run on a part-time basis; about two-thirds are less than 50 acres (20 hectares); and there are some very large-scale farms of several thousand acres.

The intensive cropping practised in the fens still requires large numbers of workers in spite of tremendous advancements in mechanisation. The pattern of the working day has not changed since the time when horses were used. The day starts at about 7 a.m., when daylight permits, and a break is made at 10.30 to 11.00 a.m. (the actual time varies considerably from parish to parish) for a meal known locally as 'dockey'. Work will then resume, with only a brief break at 1.00 p.m., until 3.00 to 3.30 p.m. As mechanisation increases and the number of workers decreases, these hours are becoming extended and it is not at all unusual to see tractors working with headlights in the dark evenings of autumn and early winter.

The main crops are cereals, sugar beet, potatoes, carrots, celery and onions, but a large number of other crops are grown on a limited scale.

Sugar beet

Sugar beet was introduced to the fens in the 1920s when processing factories were built at Ely, Wissington, King's Lynn and Peterborough. The Ely factory (closed in 1981) had a quay on the river Ouse, and when it was first built large quantities of beet were delivered by barge. Indeed, it was hoped that this new trade would boost commercial traffic on fenland rivers and help to keep them viable in the face of increased road and rail competition. For many years the Wissington factory took deliveries only by barge and rail.

It was often easier to load barges on a nearby river than to cart the beet down soft muddy droves to be sent either by rail or by road. Some of the larger farms even had railways connecting their land to the roads. It was easier for horses to pull truck loads along the railways than in ordinary farm carts, and the rail tracks could be used throughout the year, even after heavy rains when the droves were temporarily impassable.

Sugar beet growing is now highly mechanised and very little hand labour is used. Beet grow best as well spaced single plants. Precision drilling, using pelletted seed, can achieve this but the traditional method of singling by hand is still practised on some farms. Sometimes this is done by workers crawling on hands and knees along each row, singling plants and removing weeds in the process.

Potatoes

Potatoes have been the most important crop in the fens for more than a century. The peat soils were easy to work with horses, and heavy yields of good quality potatoes could be obtained without using any more manure than was made by bullocks kept to fatten in yards during the winter.

Shrinkage of peat, followed by an increasing acreage of skirtland, has made complete mechanisation difficult. Nevertheless, automatic planters, weedkillers and complete harvesters keep the hand labour to a minimum. To produce first quality potatoes of the standard required for pre-packing, great care in handling the crop is needed and hence the use of hand pickers on many of the harvesters in current use.

Varieties of potatoes grown in the fens have changed very little until recent years. King Edwards, which are grown on some farms, have no flowers but some of the newer varieties make the potato fields, for a short period in July, almost as striking as the spring bulb fields. Particularly noticeable are the purple flowers of Maris Piper which has become very popular since it was introduced on a commercial scale in the early 1970s.

The concentration of potatoes encourages epidemics of potato blight (the disease which caused the famine in Ireland in the mid 1840s) to develop quickly under suitable weather conditions. To keep losses from this disease to a minimum a routine of spraying with fungicide at weekly or ten-day intervals is followed by most farmers. The open fen fields are ideal for aerial spraying and both fixed-wing aircraft and helicopters are commonly used. Flying at only just above crop height, their presence is often unnoticed until they are overhead or making an abrupt and noisy turn on the edges of the fields.

The traditional method of storing potatoes in clamps (sometimes referred to as graves) still exists in the fens. The freshly lifted potatoes are put into long heaps, triangular in cross-section, and covered initially with straw. Later, as a protection from frost, earth is put over the straw. Some other types of store which are rectangular and not covered with earth can be seen on some farms. Known as 'Dickie pies', these rely on walls made of straw bales for protection from winter frosts. However, most potatoes are now stored in specially constructed buildings.

Carrots

Light peat soils in the Chatteris area have been the main centre of carrot growing in the fens for many years. Well shaped carrots from these soils are easy to harvest and wash for pre-packing or canning. In and around Chatteris there are a number of grower-merchants who grow carrots on land hired on a yearly basis. As the area of peat soil has fallen due to peat shrinkage and to the appearance of clay in the soil (which in turn makes washing the carrots more difficult) the carrot growers have extended their activities into the sandy lands of Norfolk and Suffolk.

Onions

Onions are a traditional crop in the Black Fen area. A large acreage of onions for pickling is concentrated in the Southery district. By using a pro-

Onion harvesting

gramme of suitable weedkillers, onions can now be produced without the need for much hand weeding which has, in the past, been a major problem. Under suitable weather conditions in the autumn, they are left in the field to ripen and dry after lifting. As high quality onions are needed for pre-packing, techniques for artifical drying have been developed at the Arthur Rickwood Experimental Husbandry Farm, Mepal, and elsewhere, so that the onion grower is no longer entirely at the mercy of the weather.

Celery

Most of the late celery produced in Britain comes from the deep peat area of the Black Fens. It is a plant which requires moisture throughout the growing season. Water can be controlled on some of the celery fields by maintaining a high level in the surrounding ditches. This is done by opening and closing sluices (or slackers) either to let in water from a main drain or to ensure that there is no excessive run-off after periods of rain.

Celery is transplanted in the early

Traditional harvesting of celery, Black Bank, Little Downham

spring by machines although until recently much was done by hand. Most of the plants are reared by specialist growers in the Whittlesey area on a contract basis. Seed is sown under glass, and then the minute seedlings are transplanted into beds where they are left until required by the main crop grower.

Cereals

Winter wheat is becoming increasingly important as a fenland crop. The peat soil does not produce good yields if a rotation of continuous cereals is followed, and hence cereals are alternated with root crops on these soils. On the heavier 'island' soils a much larger proportion of the land is devoted to cereals, and oilseed rape is often alternated with them.

Livestock

There are very few dairy herds, beef cattle or sheep in the area. A few are kept on the higher land where some of the grassland is still in 'ridge and furrow', showing that it has not been ploughed since the Middle Ages. The Washes are used for summer grazing of cattle, sheep and horses. Some of the arable by-products such as sugar beet tops are folded with fattening lambs in the autumn.

Places of Interest

Anglesey Abbey

Anglesey Abbey

At Lode there is Anglesey Abbey which, with most of its contents and a substantial endowment, was acquired by the National Trust under the will of the 1st Baron Fairhaven. An Augustine priory was established here in the 12th century and remained in holy orders until the dissolution of the monasteries in 1535. It had a number of secular owners before it was acquired in 1926 by Lord Fairhaven, who landscaped the 100 acres (40 hectares) of grounds and had the Abbey reconstructed to accommodate a large collection of works of art of many kinds.

Rose, hyacinth, dahlia, herbaceous and other gardens of a formal nature surround the Abbey, and wide tree-lined avenues traverse the grounds. A number of walks with spectacular and unusual specimen trees and statues are a special feature. A barge-boarded water-mill straddles Quy Water, which flows to the west of the gardens.

The Abbey itself houses an enormous collection of continental and Eastern works of art. The unique collection of over 100 oil-paintings and water-colours of Windsor are now housed in the upper gallery, which was specially built for this purpose in 1955 to the design of Sir Albert Richardson.

Burwell and Reach

The villages of Burwell, Reach, Swaffham Bulbeck and Bottisham all have their lodes which connect them with the river Cam. At one time these waterways were busy with barge traffic, and evidence of this is particularly obvious at 'Commercial End', Swaffham Bulbeck, where warehouses and maltings can still be recognised.

From Reach to Woodditton there is a 7-mile-long (11 kilometres) Devil's Dyke, one of the three ditches which straddle the ancient Icknield Way. It was probably dug in the 6th or 7th century as a defensive barrier. At the west end, beyond Reach, there would then have been swampy impassable fens, and to the east, a forbidding forest to deter invaders. Unusual plants such as the lizard orchid and pasque-flower grow on the chalk banks of the dyke.

Crowland

The main attraction of the small town of Crowland, situated in the northern part of the Black Fens, is the ruin of the Benedictine abbey founded by St Guthlac, a monk from Repton who, over 1,300 years ago, 'By divine guidance came in a boat to one of the solitary desert islands called Crulande, on St Bartholomew's Day and in a hollow on the side of a heap of turf built himself a hut'.

Another well-known feature is the 600-year-old triangular bridge standing in the centre of the town. Water no longer flows beneath its arches. A stone figure of Our Lord holding the world, from the abbey ruins, is thought to have been placed there in 1720.

Denver

Denver village is about one mile (1.6 kilometres) from the sluices which have already been described in the context of fenland drainage (see pp. 18-19). It has a well preserved tower windmill formerly used for grinding corn. The church and a number of the older houses are built of carstone. This material, which was used extensively for building in this part of Norfolk, is quarried in the Snettisham area. George Manby, who invented the first rocket life-saving apparatus, was born in Denver; he carried out some of his early experiments by firing rockets over the parish church.

Ely

From whichever direction Ely is approached, a part of the fens has to be crossed. Hereward the Wake, leader of the revolt against the Norman conquest of 1066, remained secure on his island hideout until William the Conqueror's army managed to find a causeway through the reedy swamp. Nobody knows for certain which route his army followed but there is a considerable body of opinion which supports the theory that he used the Aldreth causeway. His army is thought to have assembled at Belsar's Hill camp at Willingham before launching the final and decisive assault.

The origins of Ely Cathedral go back to AD 673 when Etheldreda, wife of the King of Northumbria, founded an abbey for both monks and nuns. By virtue of many endowments the abbey became very rich, and when Simon, Prior of Winchester, became Abbot of

Ely Cathedral Octagon

Ely in 1081 he planned to build a church which eventually became the Cathedral. The choir was completed in 1106, and in 1109 a Bishopric of Ely was created by Henry I.

A unique feature of the Cathedral is the octagon, built by Alan of Walsingham between 1323 and 1330. The lantern, which rises for 63 feet (19 metres), is constructed round a framework of eight massive oak beams. Below this, a network of timber beams stretches out to the supporting walls which have to bear the 400 tons (404 tonnes) of wood and lead of which the octagon is made. The genius of the medieval craftsmen can be appreciated when it is remembered that it was built over 600 years ago.

A few years ago it was discovered that death-watch beetle had largely eaten away the ends of the sixteen beams supporting the lantern. The cost of restoration, amounting to £60,000, was raised by public subscription.

A range of stones was used in building the Cathedral, most of which were obtained from quarries from which they could be transported by barge to Ely. The main stone is from Barnack, near Stamford, but some also came from Lincoln Cathedral quarries. In Burwell, Reach and Isleham there was quarried at one time a stone called 'clunch', a hard form of chalk, and it is thought that the clunch used in the Lady Chapel and elsewhere probably came from those areas. The Cathedral is built on a solid rock known as carstone, which underlies this part of Ely.

Although some repair work was carried out during the 1960s, restoration on a much more extensive scale began in 1972. The work has been made possible by generous support given to a restoration fund appeal.

Many of the remaining monastic buildings are now used by the King's School. The Ely 'Porta', which was the main entrance to the Benedictine priory, was built in 1400, and is used as an assembly room while the monks' granary is now a dining hall. As a granary it was used to store produce from various manors which, in normal years, made the monks self-sufficient.

In the shadow of the Cathedral stands the parish church of St Mary. Adjoining the churchyard is a timbered house, once the residence of Oliver Cromwell, who lived there for 11 years, during which time he was a collector of Cathedral tithes. His fourth son, Henry, lived there as a youth, and after returning as Lord Deputy of Ireland, he lived at Spinney Abbey, Wicken.

The quayside, which was once a busy trading area used by river barges, is now a popular mooring for holiday cruisers, some of which are built in the boatyard situated on the island known locally as Babylon. Here the King's School has its boathouse which is used in the early part of each year by the Cambridge crew. The crew practises on a straight stretch of the Ouse a little further downstream, before moving to the tideway in final preparation for the annual boat race against Oxford. During the Second World War the races were contested over this stretch of the river.

A riverside walk is now one of the attractive features. In 1971 some disused maltings were converted into a public hall for concerts, meetings and other functions.

Haddenham

The Farmland Museum at Haddenham displays objects connected with the domestic and farming history of the area. There is a particularly good collection of horse ploughs and other horse-drawn implements. It is open to the public some weekends.

Littleport

Although on the river Ouse, the small town of Littleport was not a port as such, the word 'port' in this context meaning 'town'. It is best known for the riots which started there in 1816. Farm workers and soldiers returning from the Napoleonic Wars found themselves unemployed at a time when the wheat price was high. They were subsisting at a near starvation level and banded together to try to get some relief from their oppression. The rioters marched to Ely, armed with bill hooks and scythes, and at the head of the column was a waggon on which fen punt guns were mounted.

They were dispersed by the military after a large number had been arrested. Many were imprisoned for a long period, five were transported to Botany Bay and five were publicly hanged. These last five are commemorated on a plaque on the west wall of the tower of St Mary's Church, Ely.

March

In his *Buildings of Cambridgeshire* (Penguin Books) Nikolaus Pevsner describes the roof of St Wendreda's church in March as 'the most splendid timber roof in Cambridgeshire'.

Wendreda is of Saxon origin and it seems likely that there has been a church on this site since that period. The present church is mainly 16th century, although the steeple, which is 140 feet (43 metres) high, dates from 1400. Medieval wood carving can be seen at its best in the elaborately decorated double hammerbeam roof. The carvings include about 120 angels. The wall posts depict the twelve apostles and at the base of these are angels, with outstretched wings, holding various musical instruments. The six bells are acknowledged as being one of the finest 'rings' in East Anglia.

Ouse Washes

There is still considerable interest in wildfowling in the Washes but in recent years the main concern has become one of conservation. The Wildfowl Trust, the Cambridgeshire and Isle of Ely Naturalists' Trust, and the Royal Society for the Protection of Birds have acquired land in the Washes which, under the management of a joint committee, is being developed as a sanctuary. The return of the black-tailed godwit, black tern and ruff as breeding species was a closely guarded secret until the new protective measures had been taken. This area is not only important as a summer breeding ground for a wide variety of species but is also a winter sanctuary for thousands of migrating ducks and swans.

During the summer a profusion of wild plants produce seed which provides the winter food for the ducks and swans attracted to the flooded Washes. Usually there is sufficient deep water for diving ducks such as pochard, while large areas which are scarcely covered by water are favoured by enormous flocks of widgeon, teal, mallard and pintail. Bewick's swans swim majestically on the wide areas of shallow lakes, while plovers and waders find food on the higher land and near the water's edge.

Regular monthly counts of wildfowl are made during the winter and on one recent occasion 42,000 widgeon, 7,000 mallard, 3,000 pintail, 5,500 pochard, 7,000 teal, 3,000 Bewick's swans, 1,100 shovellers and 900 tufted ducks were recorded on the Washes. This number of Bewick's swans represents about 25 per cent of the population of north-western Europe.

Welney Wildfowl Refuge (The Wildfowl Trust) The importance of the Ouse Washes as a wildfowl sanctuary increases as further areas of similar marshy ground, both in the British Isles and on the European continent, are drained. From funds raised through a public appeal and private donations, the Wildfowl Trust has constructed a lake where water can be maintained at a constant level by operating sluice

Welney Wildfowl Refuge:
the main observatory seen from one of the wings

gates, to attract Bewick's swans. A further inducement is provided by twice-daily feeding with wheat, barley or potatoes. Now that the swans have become accustomed to him, the warden can set out from his store and walk along the water's edge throwing out scoops of grain from his old wheel-barrow without disturbing them. But he has to wear an old coat on every occasion and his progress must be smooth and unhurried, with measured steps. Anything unusual about his dress, manner or gait sends the swans skywards into the distant washes from where they may not return for several hours.

Overlooking the lake is a centrally heated observatory from where the swans and ducks can be seen and studied at close quarters. To prolong the period for observation floodlighting is provided. As dusk begins to fall the lights are switched on, dim at first but gradually brightening until they are at full strength half-an-hour later. Bewick's swans have been the subject of detailed research at Slimbridge for many years because each has a unique marking on its beak which enables the expert eye to identify individuals. The shapes of the marks have been recorded for hundreds of swans, and most of them have been named. Each summer the swans migrate to the tundras bordering the Kara Sea in Siberia and when the autumn comes anxious eyes strain to see if 'Colonel and His Lady' will return bringing with them their cygnets. Will Punch have found Judy, and will Comet, who was alone last winter, have returned with a mate? Detailed records, which are helping to establish the habits and movements of these swans and to assess the stresses and strains of their long migratory flights, are invaluable in the development of satisfactory sanctuaries and conservation programmes.

Welches Dam The R.S.P.B. refuge with observation hides overlooking the Washes is based at Welches Dam, near Manea.

Peterborough

Peterborough Cathedral was begun in 1118 and is a fine example of Norman architecture. Queen Catherine of Aragon, first wife of Henry VIII, is buried here. Mary, Queen of Scots, was originally buried here after being beheaded at Fotheringay Castle. The museum in Priestgate has a piece of her needlework as well as a fine collection of historical items from Peterborough and the fens.

Prickwillow

At Prickwillow a disused drainage station is now open to the public under the auspices of the Prickwillow Engine Trust. The five-cylinder Murlees engine, built in 1923, was in use on this site for 50 years before being replaced by an electric pump which is housed nearby.

Other fen drainage pumps are being added to the collection which includes a display of early drainage and farming tools.

Soham

The small town of Soham was, during the Second World War, the scene of great bravery. An ammunition train with 51 waggons was near Soham when the driver noticed that the first waggon was on fire. The train was brought to a halt and the driver and fireman managed to uncouple the blazing waggon. They drove the engine and truck away but had gone only some 100 yards (91 metres) when the truck exploded, killing the fireman, fatally injuring the signalman and seriously injuring the driver. The station was completely destroyed but the town was saved.

At Fountain Lane there is a steelyard which is still in working condition.

Stretham Engine

The only steam engine preserved in the Black Fens is at Stretham where an engine was first erected in 1831. It replaced four windmills and drove a scoop-wheel of 29 feet (9 metres) in diameter with paddles 3 feet (1 metre) wide. Further peat shrinkage necessitated increasing the diameter to 33 feet (10 metres) in 1848, and for the same reason the diameter was changed again in 1896 to 37 feet (11 metres). The last wheel, which had 48 paddles each 2.5 feet (0.75 metres) wide, was able to lift 30 tons (30.3 tonnes) of water on each revolution. With a normal work rate of four revolutions it could therefore raise 120 tons (121 tonnes) or nearly 30,000 gallons (113,400 litres) of water per minute.

The Stretham engine is typical of

Stretham Engine, by the Old West River

many used in this part of the fens. It had a beam of nearly 25 feet (7.6 metres) and drive was achieved through a Watts parallel motion. It was built by Butterby and Co. at a total cost of £4,250, which included £2,050 for machinery and brickwork. To raise steam from a cold start half a ton of coal was burned and even after the valves were improved in 1909 the engine consumed one ton (almost one tonne) of coal every six hours.

Since it ceased work it has been under the care of the Stretham Engine Preservation Trust and can be seen from 8.00 a.m. to 5.00 p.m. in the summer and from 8.00 a.m. to dusk in winter. A number of old domestic utensils, fen tools and other relics are also on show.

The preservation of the engine is, to some extent, fortuitous. Many fen engines situated in low-lying areas were replaced by diesel or electric pumps. However, as Stretham was not situated at the lowest part of the area, it was not replaced with a new pump. Of the many other beam engines all that remain are the characteristic buildings which housed the beam and the scoop-wheel. In many cases the chimney has been demolished.

Thorney

Thorney is an unusual fenland parish in that it was owned for a long period by the Bedford family. The connection goes back to the reign of King Edward VI (1537-53). Lord Russell did commendable service for the King, especially in the west country where he raised the siege of Exeter and quelled a dangerous rebellion. As a token of gratitude Edward VI created him Earl of Bedford in 1550 and at the same time granted him the manors of Thorney Abbey. When leading the Adventurers in the drainage work, the 4th Earl used a number of Walloon refugees from Picardy and northern Flanders. Many of them settled in Thorney where they had their own French minister and even into the 18th century a French baptismal register was kept.

Following allocation of land after drainage had been completed, the Earl of Bedford was able to add land to his Thorney estate. When it was first acquired there were 300 acres (120 hectares) of land under cultivation, but by the 19th century the estate had grown to 23,000 acres (9,310 hectares) some of which had been subsequently purchased. Most of the farms and cottages were rebuilt during the mid 19th century and today still bear a plaque giving the date of reconstruction. Although a vast amount of money was spent on the farms and on village amenities, farming became depressed during the late 19th century and income from rents fell. In the early years of this century the 11th Duke of Bedford decided to dispose of the whole estate and thus sever the long connection with the Bedford family.

Part of the original Abbey church remains as the parish church. The nave is over 100 feet (30 metres) long but the original aisles have disappeared, as has part of the east end.

Whittlesey

Whittlesey is the centre of one of the main brick-making areas in the country. Some of the most advanced techniques are used in excavating the clay and processing it into a variety of types of bricks. A butter cross is a prominent feature in the centre of the town, and a few stretches of thatched wall, which were once very common, can still be seen.

Wicken Fen

Another National Trust property, Wicken Fen has been acquired gradually since 1899, chiefly through private gifts. It comprises about 750 acres (304 hectares) of Wicken Sedge, St Edmund's and Adventurers Fens. Since Wicken Fen has never been ploughed there has been less wastage here and paradoxically this area of natural fen is now above the level of the surrounding countryside. To preserve it in its natural state water level has to be kept high in Wicken Lode and in various dykes which cross the fen.

A routine of cutting management is now followed in parts of the area so that typical reed beds, sedge fen and fen carr (a scrubby woodland) are maintained. Reeds are cut during the winter and bundled up for sale for thatching. Limited use is also made of the sedge bundles. The existence in the carr area

Reed cutting, Wicken Fen

of buckthorn (*Rhamus cartharticus*) was of strategic importance during the Second World War as the charcoal which could be derived from it was essential for use in explosive fuses.

The various habitats provide areas of special interest to plant ecologists, and many rare plants attract the attention of systemic botanists. It was, at one time, famous for its large copper and swallow-tailed butterflies. These have not been resident in recent years although efforts are being made to reintroduce them.

This part of the fens is open throughout the year, and visitors can walk along droves through the relic fenland, and see the one remaining drainage windmill. Also of interest are some pits which originally provided clay for bricks for use in the village. These man-made pools are now covered with water-lilies during the summer and surrounded by reeds.

Adventurers Fen was reclaimed during the Second World War and used for arable farming. The struggle against water, bog oaks and other adversities is related in Alan Bloom's *The Farm in the Fen* (Faber and Faber/EP Pub-

North Brink, Wisbech

lishers). The fen has now been allowed to revert to its more natural condition, and a large artificial mere has been created, which forms an ideal habitat for wildfowl, both migrating and resident nesting species. A special hide has been built alongside Wicken Lode for bird-watchers.

Wisbech

The north side of the river Nene is well known for its Georgian houses, among which is the National Trust property, Peckover House. Built in 1722 it has some superb rococo decoration in wood and plaster.

Wisbech is a busy port, which handles principally timber, grain, oil and fertiliser. There is a museum with a fine collection of china and items of local interest.

The surrounding silt soils are used for fruit growing and nursery stock production. Strawberries and gooseberries are the main soft fruits, and Bramley apples are the most important of the wide range of top fruit grown in the area. In recent years, rose bush and nursery stock production has increased.

Fenland Waterways - Past and Present